JOSEPH MIDTHUN   SAMUEL HITI

NUMBERS

WORLD
BOOK

www.worldbook.com

World Book, Inc.
180 North LaSalle Street
Suite 900
Chicago, Illinois 60601
USA

For information about other World Book publications,
visit our website at www.worldbook.com
or call 1-800-WORLDBK (967-5325).
For information about sales to schools and libraries,
call 1-800-975-3250 (United States),
or 1-800-837-5365 (Canada).

Building Blocks of Mathematics:
  Numbers
ISBN: 978-0-7166-7896-0 (trade, hc.)
ISBN: 978-0-7166-1477-7 (pbk.)
ISBN: 978-0-7166-1875-1 (e-book, EPUB3)
ISBN: 978-0-7166-2445-5 (e-book, PDF)

Acknowledgments:
Created by Samuel Hiti and Joseph Midthun
Art by Samuel Hiti
Text by Joseph Midthun
Special thanks to Anita Wager,
Hala Ghousseini, and Syril McNally

TABLE OF CONTENTS

There is a glossary on page 30. Terms defined in the glossary are in type **that looks like this** on their first appearance.

WHAT ARE NUMBERS?

Hey there!

Numbers are what we use to talk about amounts of things.

You've heard of numbers before, right?

Numbers tell us "how many."

We can express numbers with words, gestures, or symbols.

Hey, it's number one...

...the symbol for one of something!

Howdy!

This number can show one of anything!

Like one shoe.

Or one apple.

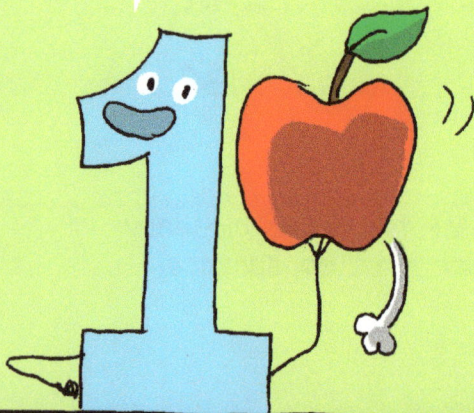

Even one number!

We have some other friends, too!

HOP

We're the **base ten** system—10 numbers that make up all other numbers!

You can use us to make any number you can think of!

Yeah, but where do we come from?

Good question!

Humans invented numbers a long time ago.

Raawwrrg!

Nope, I'm pretty sure it was humans.

We don't know *exactly* where or when numbers were invented, but we have some good clues...

EARLY COUNTING METHODS

We *do* know that people didn't always use written numbers.

They likely counted on their fingers when they were out and about.

To keep track of an amount, people etched tally marks on cave walls.

Or a piece of wood!

Or stones!

Or bones!

Each tally mark stood for *one* thing.

Much later, people invented names for different numbers.

Then they started to arrange the names in order by size.

That's counting!

At some point, ancient Egyptians started to use different objects to represent groups of 10 things.

For instance, a single stone might stand for a herd of 10 sheep.

This idea made counting large numbers of things faster and easier!

Today, we continue to represent large numbers by using groups of 10.

That's why we call ourselves the base ten **number system!**

Eventually, people developed number systems, or ways of counting and naming numbers.

The ancient Egyptians used a system based on groups of 10.

Like you, they used symbols called numerals. Each numeral represented a certain amount.

The Egyptians had special symbols for their numbers, like these:

1   10   100

They also had symbols for big numbers like 1,000.

For 1,000, the Egyptians drew a picture of the lotus flower.

TINK TINK   TINK TINK

There are thousands of lotus flowers in the Nile River, even now!

But the Greeks used the letters of their alphabet to write numbers.

Like the Egyptians, the ancient Greeks counted by groups of 10.

The first nine letters stood for ones, from 1 through 9.

A B Γ Δ E F Z H Θ I
1 2 3 4 5 6 7 8 9 10

The ancient Chinese also counted by groups of 10.

They performed calculations using rods made of animal bones or bamboo.

Early Chinese numerals looked like these rods:

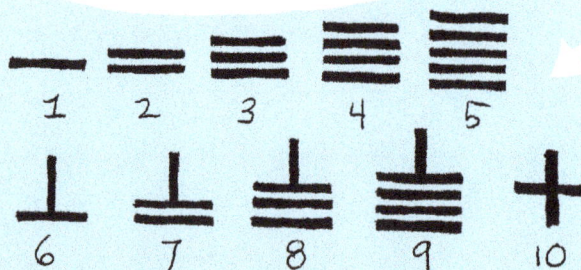

1 2 3 4 5

6 7 8 9 10

But base ten isn't the only way people counted.

The Maya of Central America counted using groups of 20.

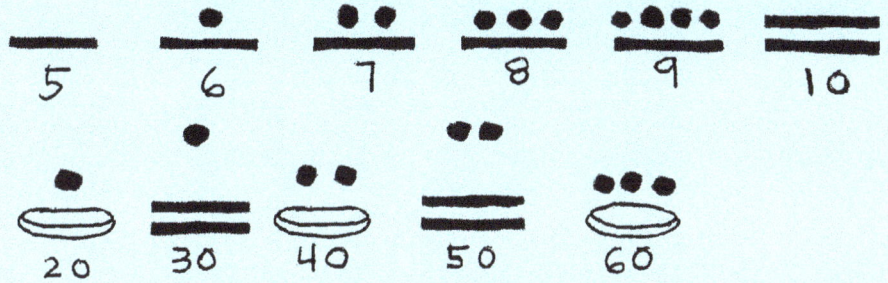

1 2 3 4

5 6 7 8 9 10

20 30 40 50 60

And the **Babylonians** of early **Mesopotamia** counted using groups of 60.

Do you notice anything odd about the symbols for 1 and 60?

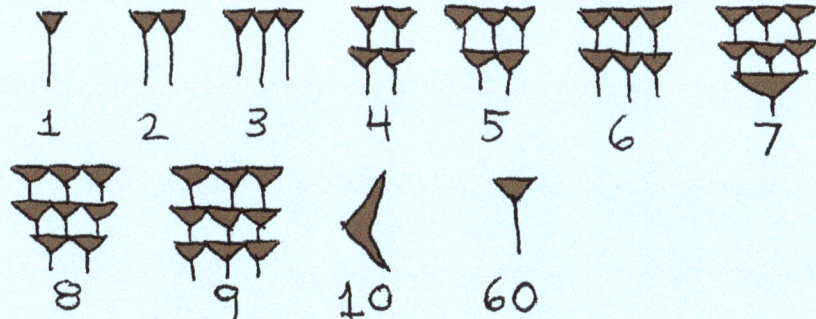

1 2 3 4 5 6 7

8 9 10 60

They're exactly the same!

1!

60!

Imagine trying to solve a math problem using the Babylonian system!

ROMAN NUMERALS

Like the Greeks, the **Romans** used letters to represent numbers.

I — 1
II — 2
III — 3
IIII — 4
V — 5
VI — 6
VII — 7
VIII — 8
VIIII — 9
X — 10

Did you know you can use your hands to make Roman numerals?

The numerals for 1, 2, 3, and 4 look like your fingers.

I II III IIII

The numeral for 5 looks like the space between your thumb and finger.

Try it!

And, the numeral for 10 looks like two crossed hands!

After a while, the Romans found a way to save time and space when writing out their numbers.

We used subtraction to make new symbols for the numbers 4 and 9.

The numeral *IIII* became *IV* and the numeral *VIIII* became *IX*...

These new symbols follow a rule:

The smaller numeral goes before the larger numeral to show that it is being subtracted.

The Romans also used other letters to stand for larger numbers...

L = 50
C = 100
D = 500

COUNTING DEVICES

People all over the world developed counting devices to help them work with large numbers.

One of the most popular early counting devices was the **abacus**.

Originally, the abacus was a tray or table covered with dust or sand.

Shake
Shake

You could make counting marks with one finger and erase them with a sweep of your hand.

Scritch

Later, people used tables marked with rows or grooves. People used pebbles or beads as counters.

The Romans even had a handheld device—a metal tray with grooves, beads, and a cover for travel.

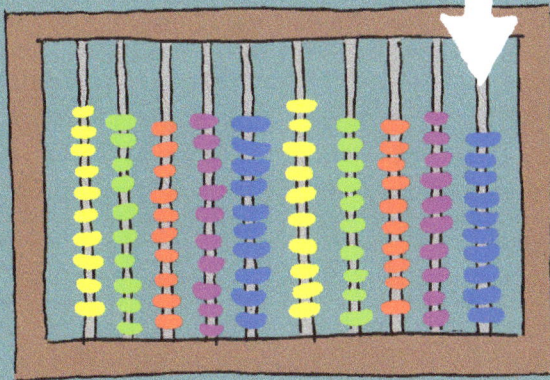

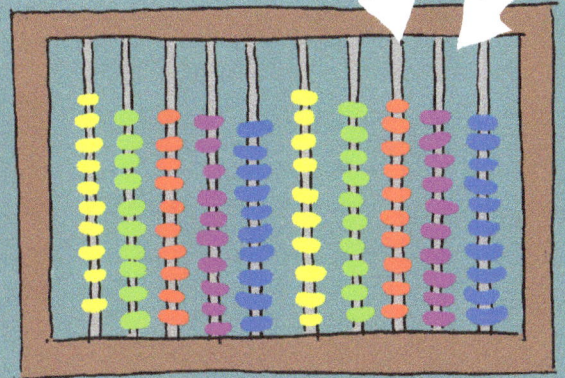

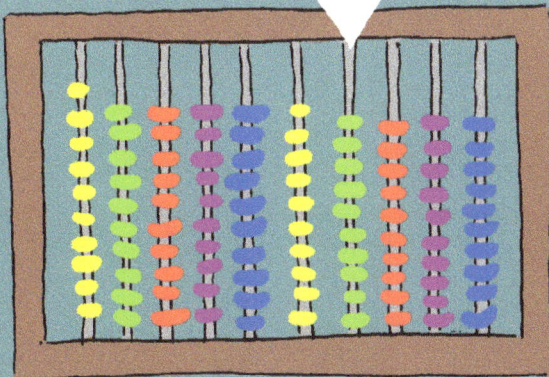

To show the 14 jars that you have, move up 4 beads in the ones column and 1 bead in the tens column.

Now, let's add the 12 jars you've decided to buy.

click click click click

Move up 2 more beads in the ones column...

...you've got: $4 + 2 = 6$.

click click

And move up 1 more bead in the tens column. Now you have:

$10 + 10 = 20$.

Click

Add the 2 tens and the 6 ones together to find out how many vegetables you have in all.

Splrrb! Glp!

That's correct!

26!

That should be plenty of veggies to make a feast!

HINDU-ARABIC NUMERALS

Take a look at these symbols for the numbers 1 through 9...

Look familiar?

In ancient times, the **Hindu** people of India used these numerals.

Over many years, and with some changes, they have become the numerals that you use today!

A.D. 100-200's	—	=	≡	Ұ	丸	丂	7	ら	?
1000's	I	Ր	ſ	κ	△	Ч	V	Λ	9
1400's	I	2	3	9	9	6	Λ	8	9
TODAY	1	2	3	4	5	6	7	8	9

The Arabs learned about these numerals and began using them, too.

After the Arabs conquered most of Spain, they brought the numerals to Europe.

Because of that, the Hindu numerals became known as Arabic numerals.

At the time, people in Europe were using Roman numerals...

...and, they continued to do so for several hundred years.

But that was all about to change.

Across Europe, mathematicians began using Hindu-Arabic numerals instead of Roman numerals.

Hmm, I wonder why...

When you're writing out equations, it's easy to make mistakes.

And using Roman numerals for large numbers can make things confusing.

Squeak

With Arabic numerals, the same equation is easier to use.

27+63

That's because the Arabic numerals have **place value!**

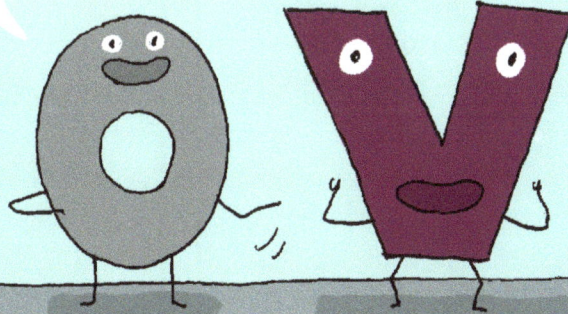

SHOWING NOTHING

Wait—I almost forgot to introduce you to one of the most important concepts of mathematics—

Me!

I'm Zero!

You use me to show *no amount*. Zip, zed, nada!

Some number systems had ways to work around using a value for nothing.

The Romans and Egyptians had symbols for 10, 100, and more. But they had nothing for me...

Showing *nothing* as a symbol proved difficult—

But I can do it!

For example, to show the number 30, you can separate 3 beads in the tens column...

...and *none* in the ones column.

CLICK

The Maya were among the first people to use symbols for the idea of zero.

Later, the Hindus found a way to show nothing.

They created a numeral and called it sunya.

Sunya stood for an empty column on an abacus.

How enlightening!

By using just 9 numerals and sunya, the Hindus could write *any* number!

The Arabs used sunya along with the other Hindu numerals.

They renamed it sifr, the Arabic word for "empty."

The Europeans adopted the numeral sifr along with the rest of the Arabic numerals.

They renamed it...

ZERO!

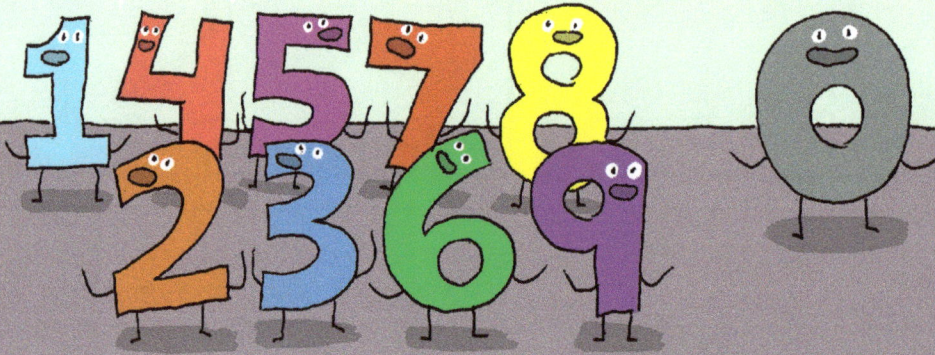

GLOSSARY

abacus a frame with rows of counters or beads used for adding and other tasks in arithmetic. The abacus was used by the ancient Greeks and Romans and in China and other Asian countries. Today, it is used in schools.

Babylonian having to do with Babylonia, an ancient region in what is now southern Iraq. Babylonia was the site of several kingdoms.

base ten a number system that uses 10 basic symbols: 1, 2, 3, 4, 5, 6, 7, 8, 9, and 0. The value of any of these symbols depends on the place it occupies in the number.

binary number a number written with only two digits: 1 and 0.

Hindu one of a group of people living in India.

number system a way of writing numbers. People in most parts of the world use the base ten number system.

place value the value of a digit as determined by its place in a number.

Mesopotamia an ancient region in the Middle East where the world's earliest cities were built.

Roman a citizen of ancient Rome.

FIND OUT MORE

BOOKS

Fun with Roman Numerals
   by David A. Adler and Edward Miller
   (Holiday House, 2008)

How Many Donkeys?
An Arabic Counting Tale
   by Margaret Read MacDonald,
   Nadia Jameel Taibah,
   and Carol Liddiment
   (Albert Whitman, 2009)

Leaping Lizards
   by Stuart J. Murphy
   and JoAnn Adinolfi
   (HarperCollins, 2005)

More or Less: A Rain Forest
Counting Book
   by Rebecca Fjelland Davis
   (Capstone Press, 2007)

On Beyond a Million:
An Amazing Math Journey
   by David M. Schwartz
   and Paul Meisel
   (Random House, 1999)

One Is a Snail, Ten Is a Crab:
A Counting by Feet Book
   by April Pulley Sayre,
   Jeff Sayre, and Randy Cecil
   (Candlewick Press, 2003)

The Story of Our Numbers:
The History of Arabic Numbers
   by Zelda King
   (PowerKids Press, 2004)

Teeth, Tails and Tentacles:
An Animal Counting Book
   by Christopher Wormell
   (Running Press Kids, 2004)

WEBSITES

1, 2, 3 Counting Games
   pbskids.org/games/counting.html
   Join your favorite PBS characters
   in learning about numbers
   and counting.

ABCya!
   www.abcya.com
   Choose your grade level to find
   number and counting games that
   are just right for you!

Count Us In
   abc.net.au/countusin
   The games and activities at this
   site are perfect for practicing
   number skills.

Gamequarium: Place Value Games
   www.gamequarium.com/placevalue.html
   This teacher-designed website
   provides many pages of games
   for practice with place value
   and other number skills.

Roman Numerals Games
   www.roman-numerals.org/games.html
   Learn about Roman numerals here
   and test your knowledge as you go!

Tamba's Abacus
   www.bbc.co.uk/cbeebies/tikkabilla/
   games/tikkabilla-tambasabacus
   Sing and count along with a
   colorful online abacus at this
   site from the BBC.

INDEX